Adventure Walks
and
Monkey Talks

Dickson H Hunley

authorHOUSE®

AuthorHouse™
1663 Liberty Drive
Bloomington, IN 47403
www.authorhouse.com
Phone: 1-800-839-8640

Published by AuthorHouse 10/19/2012

ISBN: 978-1-4772-7558-0 (sc)
ISBN: 978-1-4772-7559-7 (e)

Library of Congress Control Number: 2012918225

This book is printed on acid-free paper.

Adventure Walks and Monkey Talks

A few years ago I was lucky enough to have met someone that changed my life forever. This someone helped me learn to love and allow myself to be loved. He showed me a view of the world that I had forgotten existed. He taught me life lessons with the wisdom of a 90 year old, and he helped me remember how to smile and laugh again. For one person to have that much of an effect on another person is impressive to say the least. When that person is a 4 year old boy, it is extraordinary. His name is Jayden, and I call him my Jayden Monkey.

I met Jayden when he was only 2. I dated his mom, Juli, for a year and a half. She is fantastic. Unfortunately, things didn't work out between us. While she and I dated, I formed a great bond with Jayden. He took those tiny hands, and he gripped my heart. After she and I separated, I lost a wonderful girl and my best friend. I also lost my little man.

Time had passed after our separation. We all realized how much Jayden and I really missed each other, and how much we meant to each other. Juli allowed us to spend time together again.

Now Jayden sleeps over once a week and we have "Guy Days." Sometimes we go to the circus, the movies, the pizza place, or splash around in the pool. We do lots of different activities during our "Guy Days." Our favorite activity is going on adventure walks. We put my dog, Dash, on his leash, and we see where our feet lead us. Sometimes our walks only last 10 minutes, and sometimes we are gone for an hour or more.

My favorite part of these adventure walks is the conversations. Jayden is curious about anything and everything he encounters. Like every four year old does, he likes to ask lots and lots of questions. Some of them are easy to answer, and others require quite a bit of thought.

It is during these walks, when we were having our conversations that I realize I wasn't just teaching Jayden. He is teaching me too. He makes me think about things in ways I never have before. I remember things I had forgotten. He makes me see things I may have missed if he hasn't pointed them out to me.

I've written down 52 of the greatest lessons I've learned from Jayden. Some lessons I have learned during our walks and some of them at other times during our "Guy

Days". Now I'd like to share them with you. I hope you enjoy reading these lessons as much as I enjoyed learning them.

Feel free to read this book any way you'd like. Read it cover to cover. Read it a few lessons at a time or one lesson a day. I'd like to suggest to you how to read it and issue you a personnel challenge. I challenge you to read one lesson a week and practice that lesson for the entire week. If you accept this challenge, I promise you that not only will you be a happier person; you will make others around you happy as well. Let your happiness be infectious and spread it wherever you go.

Lesson 1

Make time to go for walks. Do it as often as you can.

Walks are a great way to get outside in the fresh air, get some exercise, explore your neighborhood, meet your neighbors, and most importantly spend time with your family. You may learn something new about your neighborhood, a loved one, and maybe even yourself. Grab the dog, the kids, and your husband or wife and get outside. There's adventure waiting for you around every corner. Are you willing and brave enough to go out there and find it? Make time to go for walks. Do it as often as you can.

Lesson 2

Be present.

Be there with your family both physically and mentally. Leave the iPod, laptop, and cell phones at home. If you have to bring your phone leave it in your pocket. Be present for your family. No distractions. Let them enjoy you, all of you, as much as you enjoy them. If you have your face in your phone texting, you will miss something. You could miss something small like a cloud shaped like an elephant or something huge like the look of wonder and excitement on your kid's face when they catch a firefly for the first time or how thrilled they are when they make the big play in the game. Don't just punch a clock and show up. Be a participant. Be present.

Lesson 3

Don't be in such a hurry.

You have your entire life to rush around and run the rat race. Go ahead and get in a rush while shopping for groceries. Hurry through the morning paper. Run from the car to your work. Hurry through everything else but slow down and enjoy the time you have with your family. This holds true in everything you do with them. Enjoy your walks together and don't rush through them. Remember, it's an adventure; not a race. Don't be in such a hurry.

Lesson 4

Be careful with your money but don't sacrifice a great experience to save a few dollars.

One of our favorite activities on our adventure walks is to feed the ducks that live on the pond where we walk. There have been times when money is tight, and I almost didn't spend the $1.58 for an extra loaf of bread to throw out to the ducks. Then I realize that the half hour of fun and laughter that Jayden and I have while feeding the ducks is more valuable than the $1.58 that the loaf of bread costs and I buy it. I'm not saying to not pay the light bill in order to buy your kid a new Xbox 360. That's irresponsible. If you can spend a few dollars for some laughter filled time with your kid, you should do it. You are a fool not to do it. Be careful with your money but don't sacrifice a great experience to save a few dollars.

Lesson 5

Look where you are going but be sure to see what is at your feet.

You have to look ahead to see where you are going, but sometimes the best stuff isn't out there ahead of you. It's right there at your feet. This can also be applied to life. Looking towards and planning for the future is necessary, but it can't be at the expense of the present. You have to appreciate what you have right here, right now. Jayden and I were taking a walk to the mail box one day. We made the trek many times. As I was looking where we were going, Jayden was looking where we were. Because he was appreciating where we were, he found a six or seven beautiful rocks. They were blue, yellow, green, and orange. They were mostly buried in the dirt. He saw them and picked them up. We took them home and cleaned them up. He then had a beautiful present to give to his mom. This wouldn't have been possible if Jayden didn't instinctively know: Look where you are going but be sure to see what is at your feet.

Lesson 6

Don't feed the monkey pizza
rolls.

This one is just for me. It serves as a constant reminder that when he eats pizza rolls he becomes a stinky butt. What comes from his behind can clear a room. If it weren't so toxic it might be considered hilarious. I beg you. Please. DO NOT FEED THE MONKEY PIZZA ROLLS.

Lesson 7

If your kid asks you to pick them up, hold them, or carry them – you do it.

Sometimes Jayden gets a little tired on the way back from a walk. Sometimes he just wants to be close to me. When this happens he'll ask me to carry him or give him a piggy back ride. He's a big kid and he gets heavy fast, but I never turn him down. He is getting so big so fast I don't know how much longer it will be before I won't be able to pick him up at all. I treat each time like it is my last. I know I still have some time before he will be too big to pick up, but there is no reason not to cherish each time like it's the last. If your kid asks you to pick them up, hold them or carry them – you do it.

Lesson 8

If you are hurtful, rude, or mean to someone today don't expect them to be there for you tomorrow.

There were two kittens abandoned in front of my apartment. I had them spayed and neutered, brought them in until they were big enough to take care of themselves, and then let them be outdoor cats. Jayden loves animals. He wanted to play with these kittens, but he was very young when we first found them and played with them a little too rough. Now they will only come close to him when we are outside playing or on an adventure walk. They come close but they won't get close enough for him to pet them. He always asks why. I have to explain to him that they are still scared of him because he used to play with them just a little too rough, and they think he will do it again. The people in your life are just like Jayden and the kittens. If you are hurtful, rude, or mean to someone today don't expect them to be there for you tomorrow.

Lesson 9

Little messes are just that, little messes.

On occasion Jayden will spill his drink or drop a bowl of strawberries. It makes a little mess, and he will apologize emphatically. Once I let him know it is ok, he helps me clean it up. Don't let a little mess turn into a big problem. Don't let it upset you and frustrate you to the point of yelling at your kid. If cleaning up a small mess is the worst thing to happen to you that day, then you are having a pretty great day. Don't let the little messes become huge problems and ruin your day. Little messes are just that, little messes.

Lesson 10

There is always a photo opportunity.

Always carry a camera with you and take lots of pictures and videos. This is very easy in our time of technology. Cameras are embedded into everything. You are rarely without one. (Just wait until the walk is over to share your pictures via email or your social networks. Remember lesson 2: be present.) Take lots of pictures and video to preserve as many moments as you can. No one has ever said "Man, I am so upset that I took all those pictures of my kid's 1st birthday party." You don't even have to buy film or pay to have it developed anymore, so cost is not an excuse to not take pictures. It's all on you. You have to do it. You'll be glad you did it. After all, you can use those pictures of you kid potty training or naked in the bathtub to embarrass them in front of his or her prom date. Pictures will bring you so much joy on so many levels. There is always a photo opportunity.

Lesson 11

Let your kid be a kid.

At times I've caught myself telling Jayden to stop, be quite, sit still, don't do that, quit running, and put that baby alligator down. We have a responsibility to teach our kids how to behave, to share, to be respectful, to be polite, and many other lessons. We don't need to teach them these things at the expense of their childhood. Life and responsibilities will come along soon enough to take away their childhood. They will be studying for the ACT instead of finger painting a picture of the family. They will be going to their part time job so they can buy a new stereo for the car you gave them on their 16th birthday instead of chasing down the ice cream truck. They will be going off to college instead of going down for a nap. Don't take his or her youth away from them prematurely. Let your kid be a kid.

Lesson 12

Keep Kleenex in your pocket.

Kleenex is a great tool for lots of situations. They are great to clean dirt and chocolate from your kids face. You can use them to dry off their hands if the paper towel dispenser in the restroom is empty. Kleenex is good at cleaning up skinned knees and elbows, as well as, wiping away tears. Last but not least, it will save you from having to use your shirt as a handkerchief. Kids' noses seem to run from age 2 until they are well in to their late teens. You're going to need something to clean them up. Keep Kleenex in your pocket.

Lesson 13

Sometimes the little questions
are the hardest ones to answer.

The hardest question is usually asked the most often. It is only one little three letter word. "Why?" Jayden likes to understand everything. I mean EVERYTHING. He digs and digs for answers until he can fully understand what he is asking. He will ask question after question in his quest to learn, and we always land on that one question that often stumps me. Why? I do my best to answer him honestly and to the best of my knowledge. There are times that the answer escapes me, and I have to be honest and tell him that I don't know. Don't let not knowing discourage you. Take this opportunity to learn something with your kid. Share that learning moment together. Find the answer on the internet. Look for answers in an encyclopedia. Take a trip with your kids to the library and do some research and reading together. Sometimes the little questions are the hardest ones to answer.

Lesson 14

Sharing is caring.

Jayden is one of the most generous people I have ever met. His mom teaches him a lot of great things, and this is one of my favorites. She has done a fantastic job of instilling the sharing is caring idea in him. He'll be the first one at lunch to tell you how good his sandwich is and offer you a bite. He divides up his toys during playtime and usually gives me "the best guys" when we are playing super heroes. In this "me first" society I think a lot of us have forgotten the joy of making someone else happy. He hasn't forgotten it and practices it every day. Make someone else feel good today. Sharing is caring.

Lesson 15

Say hello to everyone and talk
to them.

Don't just talk to them. Show interest in them. You might learn something from them. Jayden walks up to lots of people and talks to them while we are out. He will ask them things like what their dog's name is, how there day is, and what they are doing? He doesn't have an agenda. He is genuinely interested in other people and wants to hear about THEM. How many people do that these days? Most people ask you a question and wait for you to finish just so they can talk about themselves. Take time to listen to someone today. Say hello to everyone and talk to them.

Lesson 16

When you laugh, laugh out loud
for everyone to hear.

I don't think Jayden has ever just chuckled. He throws his head back and laughs from deep down in his belly, which he is usually holding. He isn't concerned that he might be disturbing someone with the noise of his laughter. He knows that laughter is a joyous sound that should fill the air and never be stifled. When did we forget this simple truth? Why did we forget it? Don't be shy about your laughter. When you laugh, laugh out loud for everyone to hear.

Lesson 17

The only thing better than playing with your kid is playing with your kid and your dog.

A boy + a ball + a dog + an open field = hours of laughter and joy. Jayden, Dash, and I do a lot of things together and playing ball is our favorite. There are only a few things, if any, that are better than watching your kid and your dog play and romp. If you had to say exactly who is enjoying it more, you would be hard pressed to choose. Kids and dogs are natural companions, and the world is a better place for it. If you have the time and means to get a dog for your kid, do it. You are missing out if you don't. The only thing better than playing with your kid is playing with your kid and your dog.

Lesson 18

Your kid is the best at every game you play with them.

I don't know how he does it but every time we race, play a game, or have any sort of competition Jayden always wins. It's usually a nail biter but he always pulls it out in the end. Seeing the smile on his face and pride in his walk after a win is just what I need to give me consolation over my loss. Your kid is the best at every game you play with them.

Lesson 19

Rides in the car are a great time
to be creative.

It can be easy to strap in the kid, turn up the radio or pop in a DVD, and just drive to your destination. Don't waste this time together. When we are stuck in the car, we like to play a rhyming game, make up songs, or tell stories. Listening to your kid sing is one of the greatest sounds you'll ever hear, but listening to them sing a song that you are creating together in the moment always sounds so much better. The stories you create together will be better than any book you will ever share. Rides in the car are a great time to be creative.

Lesson 20

Shower your kids with affection
and be sure to save some for
mom.

If it weren't for mom you wouldn't have those kids that bring you so much joy. Be sure to make some time for her. She needs and deserves as much affection as the kids. Showing your love for the kids does not equate to showing your love for mom. She wants her own special attention. If you think about all she does for you and the family you'll agree that she more than deserves it. Shower your kids with affection and be sure to save some for mom.

Lesson 21

If you aren't involved with your kids' mom you must speak highly of her or not at all when you're with the kids.

You may not care for each other but you shouldn't speak poorly of each other in front of the kids. You thought very highly enough of each other at one point for a few minutes at least. If you didn't then there wouldn't be any kids between the two of you. Try to focus on those good times when talking to the kids about mom. If you aren't involved with your kids' mom you must speak highly of her or not at all when you're with the kids.

Lesson 22

Hugs – give them out often and abundantly. Bring it in!

There aren't many situations that can't be made better by a hug. Jayden is a great hugger and he isn't shy about giving them out. He throws his arms out wide and says "Bring it in." My favorite hug I get is when I go to pick him up and he runs to me and jumps in my arms and squeezes me really tightly. In that moment everything is right in the world and there is no place I'd rather be. Think about how great it feels to have someone you love wrap their arms around you, squeeze you close, and make you feel cared for and warm. You're smiling right now just thinking about that feeling, aren't you? Don't you want to give that feeling to the ones you care about the most? Hugs – give them out often and abundantly. Bring it in!

Lesson 23

Dress how you want to dress. Make your own fashion statement.

Too often people are worried about what others will think when they choose how to dress. Jayden is not a slave to what society considers fashionable. He wears what he likes and what is comfortable. He wears his shorts backwards. He wears colors that don't match. He'll put on a striped shirt with plaid shorts. He's not caught up with how other people look at his clothes. He's happy and he's free. You should feel that way too. Dress how you want to dress. Be free. Make your own fashion statement.

Lesson 24

Try things for the 1st time for a 2nd time.

I used to despise bologna. I loathed it. It was my mortal enemy. My Jayden Monkey loves pabloney. You didn't read that wrong. He calls it pabloney. He likes to have pabloney and cheese sandwiches for lunch. When he asks me to have one with him I can't refuse. Guess what? I don't hate it anymore. I actually like it. This made me rethink all the things I've previously disliked. I've given quite a few things a second chance and found out that my opinion of them has changed. I enjoy things now that I previously disliked. Give some of the things that you have written off another chance. You may just find out that you like them now. Try things for the 1st time for a 2nd time.

Lesson 25

Your parents are laughing at
you.

Your kids won't believe it, but you had a different life before they were born. During your life before them, you had quite a few experiences that have taught you a lot of things. Now, you're a little bit older a whole lot wiser. Age and experience have been great to you. Even with all that experience there are times that your kids still won't want to listen to you. It's frustrating isn't it? Good thing you always listened to your parents. You DID listen to everything your parents said, right? Remember what they used to say to you? "When you have kids I hope they turn out just like you." Your parents are laughing at you every time you get frustrated because your kids don't listen or act up. Let them laugh. They've earned it. When they are done laughing and have finally caught their breath, go ahead and ask them for help with any problem you have. They'll have the answer because they have more life experiences than you; they are older and wiser than you and have been a parent much longer than you. They love you and they love to help you. Your parents are laughing at you.

Lesson 26

Be polite. Please and thank you
are not dirty words.

There's an old proverb that says courtesy costs nothing but gains everything. Jayden is a very polite kid but sometimes he forgets to say please and thank you. I remind him and he is always quick to say the magic words. What's better than that is when I forget he will remind me. Why do we sometimes forget? Is it that hard to be polite to people? Why are we stingy with our manners? Make a pledge to be polite, especially to the ones you love. Be polite. Please and thank you are not dirty words.

Lesson 27

You're going to watch a lot of Sponge Bob. Embrace it.

You probably don't like Sponge Bob and want to watch the local news or reruns of Friends. You're not going to get to do that. Sponge Bob is on. As a parent you're going to have to do a lot of things that you don't like. You're going to do those things because you're a great parent, and you want to make your kid happy no matter the personal sacrifice. I suggest you turn into it the skid. Do whatever it takes to enjoy it. I used to hate Sponge Bob. Now I sit on the couch with Jayden, and we are both laughing. You'll enjoy the time with your kid more if you find a way to enjoy what they enjoy and bond with them over it. You're going to watch a lot of Sponge Bob. Embrace it.

Lesson 28

Sooner or later the kids want to take off the water wings and jump in the deep end.

It's terrifying, and you are a nervous wreck the whole time. You have to let them do it. You can't hold them back. You might have to pay closer attention to them when you go to the pool, but the new adventure is worth it. You should take off the water wings and jump in the deep end occasionally in your life too. You should take a risk every now and then to add some excitement to your life. Do something to get your heart racing. Take a trip outside of your comfort zone. Your life will be richer for the experience. Sooner or later the kids want to take off the water wings and jump in the deep end.

Lesson 29

Cook with your kids.

Jayden and I have the best time in the kitchen and he is a great helper. There are so many things you can teach you kids in the kitchen. You can teach them hot and cold, shapes, measurements, tell them about germs, and how to handle sharp cooking utensils safely to name a few things. By spending time in the kitchen with your kids, you can start healthy eating habits early. You can teach them your favorite recipe, create a new favorite recipe together, and show them how to use the best ingredient of all – love. Cook with your kids.

Lesson 30

Not all treasures are shiny.

Jayden and I find treasures all the time. Sometimes it's a stick that makes a really good walking stick. Sometimes it's a beautiful flower for mom. Sometimes its shiny rocks that we pretend are precious jewels. You couldn't get a dollar for all of the treasures that we have found together, but to us they are priceless. You can find priceless treasures every day too. Just look around. They aren't hard to find. The sound of your kid breathing while they sleep, the twinkle in your special someone's eye when they wink at you, the smile you get when you think about him or her. All of these things are treasures, and they should be appreciated and cherished. Find the everyday treasures in life and hold on to them. Your life will be rich and fruitful if you do. Not all treasures are shiny.

Lesson 31

If you see a pretty flower you have to pick it and give it to mom. No exceptions.

Jayden loves to pick flowers for his mom. When he sees flowers, he's picking the prettiest of the bunch and his mom is getting a beautiful bouquet. It shouldn't take your kids picking flowers for you to remember to show your appreciation for mom. Make her favorite dinner for her. Tell her to go out for a girls' night out while you watch the kids. Call the babysitter and take her out on the town. Give her flowers. Give her a compliment. Give her a kiss on the cheek. Give her a smack on the butt. Tell her you love her. Tell her you need her. Tell her want her. Tell her how much you appreciate her. Show her how much you appreciate her. If you see a pretty flower you have to pick it and give it to mom, no exceptions.

Lesson 32

Dirt under your fingernails isn't always a bad thing.

Jayden is four years old and he loves to play outside. He gets dirty and he often has dirty fingernails. It's true that dirty nails are not welcome at all times and acceptable for every occasion. If you encounter someone with dirt under their nails, don't be too quick to judge. There are many people who work very hard to support their family, and they get dirty sometimes. Don't look down your nose at someone because they get dirty at work. Look at them with the respect they deserve because they work hard every day doing a job most won't do to support themselves and the family that they love. Hard working men and women are some of the greatest people you will ever be lucky enough to meet. Dirt under your fingernails isn't always a bad thing.

Lesson 33

Saying goodbye is never easy so say it from the heart.

I love seeing the look of excitement on Jayden's face when I drop him off with Juli. He loves his mom and watching them being reunited is heartwarming. Saying goodbye to my little man is heart breaking...EVERY TIME. When I leave, I start counting down the minutes until I get him again. Life is crazy, and you never know when you will be saying goodbye to someone for the last time. When you leave someone, don't leave any question as to how you feel about them. Squeeze them tight. Tell them that you love them. Give them a kiss. Never leave them wondering. Never leave regretting you didn't tell them how much they mean to you. Saying goodbye is never easy so say it from the heart.

Lesson 34

Take new roads.

Lesson 36

Try the veal. I'll be here all week.
You have to have a sense of
humor.

Sometimes I meet Jayden's mom at a locati
out of the way for either of us so I can drop
off. One day on the way to our usual meeting
and I took a new route. We got to check o
scenery and we found a way that got us the
can't always go down the same paths, take t
and get stuck doing the same old routine i
to mix it up once in a while. You have to ac
life. Go out and find new adventures. Take

re
s.
n.
ns
ho
en
or
of
to
e...
And
n.

Having a sense of humor will make your trip through life so much more enjoyable. You can be a beacon of light and hope if you can find the humor in situations where others are finding stress and losing patience. A well timed joke or humorous observation can take the tension out of a room and lighten the mood. There is enough negativity out there in the world waiting to drag people down. Don't you add to it. Try the veal. I'll be here all week. You have to have a sense of humor.

Lesson 37

You have to reprimand your kids.
You owe it to them.

This is hard to do for me because I'm not Jayden's dad but I have a responsibility to him, his mom, his grandparents and society to teach him right from wrong when the situation arises. It's heartbreaking when your kid gets mad at you because you have to reprimand them. Just know that heartbreak will be replaced with pride when you see that your kids retained what you taught them and they do the right thing the next time the same situation presents itself. It's great to be your kids' friend but you have to be their parent first. You have to reprimand your kids. You owe it to them.

Lesson 38

You don't always have to be a
rock.

It's good to be strong and to be able to do things on your own. It's also perfectly fine to ask for help. I am one of the most stubborn and hard-headed individuals you will ever encounter. I've always been on my own, and I'm accustomed to doing things by myself. Once Jayden came in to my life, I quickly discovered that no matter how badly I wanted to do it all on my own, I had to ask for help from time to time. I've been very blessed to have some very smart and loving people in my life like my mom, my sister, Jayden's grandma and grandpa, and most of all Juli to help me. They give me help or answer questions when I need it. I felt bad bothering them at first, but soon I realized that they didn't see it as a bother. They are glad to help. I've found that I'm much happier and more successful when I am part of a team and not standing alone. You don't always have to be a rock.

Lesson 39

Be curious and ask lots questions.

Why are we scared to ask questions? What is there to be embarrassed about when trying to find answers? Why are we more concerned about what people will think of us about asking a question than we are about getting a correct answer? Jayden doesn't care what people think about him asking questions. He just wants to learn. If he thinks you have an answer to one of his questions he isn't going to shy away from you. He's going to speak up and ask you. Don't let your ego get in the way of your learning. Be curious and ask lots questions.

Lesson 40

Talk to your kids like they are adults.

Sure they're small, loud, and dirty little people that sometimes smell funny, but they are just that: little people. Don't patronize them when you talk to them. Stop using the little kid voice. You may have to explain more things to them than you planned, but your kid will benefit from it. If you don't talk down to your kids, you will expose them to a larger vocabulary and help them to learn and grow. You can paint a picture for your kids with your words. Don't limit the colors in the pallet that you paint that picture with. Talk to your kids like they are adults.

Lesson 41

Be compassionate.

Jayden likes to save the drowning bugs in the pool. If another kid is crying he asks why and wants to help. If you are feeling down he gives you a hug. He likes to make people feel better and to help them when they need it. When he does this, he's not looking for anything in return. He just wants to make others feel better. We should all strive to be more like him. Let's do something to make another feel better without looking for or expecting a reward today. Be compassionate.

Lesson 42

If you don't bother them, they won't bother you.

Jayden loves animals, and he loves to ask questions about them. When he sees an animal on TV, in a book, or if we are on a walk he asks "What can that do to you?" He wants to know if it can bite, scratch, peck, or hurt him in any way. I tell him what to look out for on each animal. I tell him that with most animals if you don't bother them, they won't bother you. I take the same approach towards people. If there is someone who will bite, scratch, peck, or hurt me, I will leave them alone. If someone can't be a positive person and always tries to drag those around them down with their negativity, I will leave them alone. By choosing not to interact with poisonous animals or people, I have never been bitten. If you don't bother them, they won't bother you.

Lesson 43

Be brave.

Being a growing boy Jayden has to do a lot of things for the 1st time. He takes on most challenges bravely. With some challenges he needs a little coaxing and support. Either way he takes those challenges head on. He breaks new personal barriers almost every day. You have to be brave too. You might not have to break through personal barriers every day, but you have to stand up and face the challenges of the day every morning. You can't cower in the corner if you want to leave your mark in life. Stand up and be bold. Leave a great legacy. Be brave.

Lesson 44

You have to communicate.

I'll ask Jayden to do something, and he will do the best job he can. He doesn't always do it 100% correctly because I never taught him how to do it. I can't get upset with him because I never told him the right way to do the job. People aren't mind readers. You have to tell them what you want, and you have to ask them what they want. If you don't talk to people, you can't get upset with them for not doing exactly what you want. I believe people naturally want to do their best, and if you're important to them they want to make you happy. You can easily help them accomplish those goals. You have to communicate.

Lesson 45

Hey! There's my imagination. It's so good to see you again.

Why is the imagination one of the first things to go when adulthood and responsibility takes over? We can get so caught up in our lives that we can lose touch with our creative and playful side. Jayden has a fantastic imagination, and he uses it all the time. Fortunately for me he has helped me rediscover my imagination. Now that my imagination and I have been reacquainted, I don't plan to ever let it go again. It's too important to misplace. Your imagination allows you to dream. It gives us hope. It turns some blankets and some pillows in to a castle that you have to defend from a hoard of attacking monsters. It brings smiles and cheers everywhere you take it. Do whatever you have to do to reignite your imagination and give it whatever it takes to fuel it. Hey! There's my imagination. It's so good to see you again.

Lesson 46

Putting the needs of someone
else first is very rewarding.

I've been on my own the majority of my adult life, so I've never had to look out for anyone else. To be honest, it wasn't all bad. Jayden came in to my life, and I had a change in my life view and shift in my priorities. Life has gotten so much better. I now have a reason to try to save money, go to bed early, to work harder and keep the house organized. When you do things like this, it doesn't feel like you are giving anything up because you are doing right by your kid. That is more than enough reward. You don't have to have a kid to put someone else's needs first. You can help a friend move instead of watching the game. You can volunteer at the animal shelter instead of spending the afternoon shopping. You can help your technologically challenged friend install a wireless router and pass on an afternoon of playing Angry Birds. Do something for a friend or better yet do something for a complete stranger today. Putting the needs of someone else first is very rewarding.

Lesson 47

It doesn't take a lot of money
to share time with your kid and
show them that you love them.

Let's face it. Kids are expensive. The burden on your wallet is heavy, but it is far outweighed by the joy you get from having kids in your life. Jayden likes going to the movies, the water park, and the pizza place like any other kid. I don't regret a penny that I've spent on my Monkey, but there isn't always money in the budget for those things. We are masters of making a lot of fun out of nothing at all. Left over bubble wrap has entertained us for an entire afternoon. A coloring book and crayons have helped us pass lots of time together. We sit side by side at the edge of the pond and fish and talk for hours at a time. None of these things are glamorous and all are very inexpensive or free. What's important is that we are spending time together. It doesn't take a lot of money to share time with your kid and show them that you love them.

Lesson 48

Oh, Karma…You're a crafty minx.

I never had any desire to date a single mom. I might have been afraid of the added commitment or maybe I didn't want to share the attention. I don't know what my issue was but I had one. Fortunately I was lucky enough to have Jayden's mom come in to my life and change my mind. She got me over my prejudice. If it weren't for her opening my eyes, I never would have met Jayden, and I wouldn't be as happy as I am today with him in my life. Now that he is in my life, I have had trouble meeting women. I'm up front with women, and I tell them that I have my little man in my life and that he is my top priority. Sometimes I can't even finish before they hit the ground running. Now I know how it feels to be the one with the kid who is being discriminated against. Dating has not been easy. Be careful about how you treat the people you have prejudices against. It may come back to haunt you. Oh, Karma...You're a crafty minx.

Lesson 49

Leave the bad stuff in the past.

Jayden and I don't always see eye to eye. There are times when we bump heads. When the dust settles and we have resolved our disagreement, we move ahead. You can't dwell on the past. You can't leave your problems unresolved either. Settle the problem at hand. Learn from it so you can avoid repeating it, and then move on and leave that problem in the past. If you rehash the same problems over and over, you will never make any forward progress. Your focus on the negative will cost you a lot of joy now and in the future. Leave the bad stuff in the past

Lesson 50

No quitting.

When Jayden tries new things he doesn't always take right to them, and he struggles. He will get frustrated and want to quit. We have a motto – No quitting. We will take on the task at hand until we have succeeded. When we have completed what we started, we celebrate. Not everything you do in life is going to be a cake walk. Life can be hard. You can't give up, especially on something that you really want. The struggle will make you appreciate it that much more when you finally accomplish your goal. No quitting.

Lesson 51

Lead by example. Be the person you want your kids to grow up to be.

You want your kid to grow up and be a wonderful person. You want them to be to responsible, well educated, and honest people who care about others and their community. Turning your kid into that adult you want is very easy. You have to be that person yourself and be a living example. Kids don't follow the 'Do as I say, not as I do' motto very well. They are little parrots who will mimic your every action. Be the best you that you can be and your kids will grow to be great adults. Lead by example. Be the person you want your kids to grow up to be.

Lesson 52

Keep learning and try to do new things with your kids.

Extracurricular learning isn't always easy. You might not have a lot of extra free time between work, school, volunteering, and being a parent. Sometimes when you are tired, being creative and coming up with new things to do with the kids can be hard. Fortunately there are books, magazines, local groups, Facebook pages, websites, and countless other resources you can use to help you out. You don't have to spend hours a day doing research. You can sign up to receive emails that you can quickly read or glance over an article while you're eating lunch. Keep learning and try to do new things with your kids.

I'm sure you will find and research resources on your own if you haven't already. If you haven't here are a few of my favorites along with a few that my friends recommend.

www.allprodad.com
www.facebook.com/MarriageWorks
www.usa.gov/Topics/Parents.shtml
www.moms.meetup.com/
www.parenting.com/
www.cafemom.com
www.webmd.com/parenting
www.parentsconnect.com/

Conclusion

I'm not trying to tell you how to be a parent or raise your children. I don't have kids of my own, so I don't feel like I have the experience to dare do such a thing. I only hope to inspire you to spend more time with your kids and most importantly, listen to them and learn from them as well as teach them. You only get a short amount of time with them. Life doesn't have a pause button. The good news is that it is never too late to start making wonderful memories. What are you waiting for? Please, take time to walk with them and talk with them. It won't be long before they don't want to spend every waking moment at your side. Those days will come much too quickly. Cherish the days you have and make the most of them.

I'd like to echo the challenge I gave you at the beginning of the book. I challenge you to read one lesson a week and practice that lesson for the entire week. If you accept this challenge, I promise you that not only will you be a happier person; you will make others around you happy as well.

Let your happiness be infectious and spread it wherever you go.

Thank you for allowing me to share just a few of the lessons that I have been lucky enough to learn while spending time with a kid that I love so very much. I appreciate your time and your attention and I wish you nothing but success and happiness for you and your family.

Acknowledgements

I have to first thank my dad, Dickson Hunley Sr., for being the greatest man I have ever met and for teaching me how to be a man. He is gone but will never be forgotten. His teachings will stick with me forever. I love you, dad.

I have to thank my mom, Darlene Hunley, for being my rock and showing me unconditional love even when I didn't always deserve it. I love you so much, mom.

I owe a huge debt of gratitude to Jayden's mom, Juli. She is always a fountain of fun, smiles, and positivity. She is one of the strongest women I know, and I can't appreciate what she has done for me enough. There are very few, if any, women who would allow an ex-boyfriend to let her son still remain a part of his life. Juli not only allows it, but she encourages it. I can't thank her enough for what she has done for me and will never be able to repay her for what she has given me. Thank you, Juli. Thank you from the bottom of my heart.

Finally I have to thank Jayden. You are a constant source of joy, love, happiness, laughter, and smiles. I will never be able to express to you how much you mean to me, and I can never repay what you have done for me. You are my inspiration for everything I do. I only hope that I can be a positive influence on you. One day, I hope that I can teach you as much as you have taught me. I love you Monkey!

Contact Dickson

If you would like to stay current with Dickson and be the first to know about his latest projects please visit www.DHH2.com

Keep up with Dickson's day to day activities. Join us on Twitter and Facebook:
Twitter www.twitter.com/DHH2Ent
Facebook www.facebook.com/DHH2Enterprises

If you are interested in having Dickson speak with your group or at your function please contact him at Info@DHH2.com